Serial Killers True Crime

Homicidal Maniacs, Bloodthirsty Serial Killers And Lethal Murderers: True Crime Stories Of Crazed Killers

This document is geared towards providing exact and reliable information in regards to the topic and issue covered. The publication is sold with the idea that the publisher is not required to render accounting, officially permitted, or otherwise, qualified services. If advice is necessary, legal or professional, a practiced individual in the profession should be ordered.

- From a Declaration of Principles which was accepted and approved equally by a Committee of the American Bar Association and a Committee of Publishers and Associations.

The information provided herein is stated to be truthful and consistent, in that any liability, in terms of inattention or otherwise, by any usage or abuse of any policies, processes, or directions contained within is the

Cover image courtesy of Daniel Hollister - https://www.flickr.com/photos/dhollister/2596483147/ and
https://www.flickr.com/photos/cogdog/8431502575/

Table of Contents

Introduction   vi

Chapter 1: Thomas the Executioner – Thomas
Neill Cream   1

Chapter 2: The Diet Hazzard   21

Chapter 3: The Moorhouse Murders   31

Chapter 4: Robin's Fetish   42

Chapter 5: Was Martha Guilty?   58

Conclusion   71

Other Books Written By Me   72

Like FREE books?

Would you like them delivered to you every week?

Do you like non-fiction books on a huge range of different topics?

We send out FREE e-books every week so we can share our books with the world!

We have FREE books every week on AMAZON that we send to our email list.

So if you want in, then visit the link at the end of this book to sign up and sit back and wait for new books to be sent straight to your inbox!

Introduction

I want to thank you for purchasing the book, *"Serial Killers True Crime: Homicidal Maniacs, Bloodthirsty Serial Killers And Lethal Murderers: True Crime Stories Of Crazed Killers"*.

Criminality is a cornucopia of irony. Although there are genes in our body which can determine our height, the color of our hair, and the complexion of our skin, there isn't one that can predispose a person's criminality. A lot of people say that background and upbringing play a huge role - and experts tend to agree.

For instance, Henry Lee Lucas' crime was said to be because of his monster of a mother. However, people with good upbringings can also turn into serial killers, such as Jesse Pomeroy, whose parents were well employed and were in a healthy, loving relationship.

It's confusing to say the least; the number of factors can't be confined to background and upbringing - there are also the issues of mental illness, lack of education, hatred towards a certain group of people, and distortion of what they believe, as was the case with Robin Gecht who used Satan as his reason to amputate human breasts.

One can fear a person and be more cautious when around him or her because that individual gives off "bad vibes", but no one can be truly sure whether he was a killer or not- until the time he was caught.

In this book, we will discuss 5 serial killers and will try to understand what drove them to perform their heinous crimes.

Thanks again, I hope you enjoy this book!

Chapter 1: Thomas the Executioner – Thomas Neill Cream

The era of 1800s was a period of development. People were in a continuous cycle of furthering their knowledge about art, science, and literature. All around the world (and especially in the Western countries), improvements in research and technology was being performed. The invention of machines, the discovery of cures and the mastery of crafts - all these and more were the focus of the generation.

Another notable change during this Victorian era was the role of women. They started demanding more rights to be in the front line of almost everything, from business to career and professions, intending to prove to the male populace that women were as capable as they were.

And true enough, the 1800s was the period of acknowledgment for many females including Dorothea Dix (an advocate for mental asylums and poorhouses), Elizabeth Blackwell (first female physician in the US), Pearl S. Buck (an author who, in 1938, won the Nobel Prize in Literature), and Florence Nightingale (the founder of modern nursing).

In all these changes, one person became hateful of the woman's battle for greatness. It was unclear where he got the notion, but Jack the Ripper intensely believed that women were an abomination to the entire human race. Experts suggested that the Doctor of Death, Thomas Neill Cream still wasn't accustomed to the idea of empowered females; hence, he performed his heinous murders, commonly through the use of strychnine poisoning.

If for one moment you felt that his method of murders denoted sympathy, to make the deaths as swift and as painless as possible, you were wrong. Strychnine poisoning to date is still one of the cruelest ways to die. The poison, be it inhaled, absorbed, or ingested, will cause a person to have continuous spasms all throughout his or her body, until the last intake of breath. For Dr. Thomas Neill Cream, this was how all women deserved to die.

Thomas and His Medical Quests

Originally from Glasgow, Thomas moved to Quebec, Canada in the year 1954, when he was just 4 years old. His father worked in the lumber industry and prospered there. All his male children followed his footsteps and succeeded, except for Thomas, the eldest, who seemed to be engrossed in books rather than the woods.

No reports of abuse or maltreatment dotted his early life, a fact which was further proven when he graduated from the acclaimed McGill's University in Montreal in 1876 with a degree of MDCM or Doctor of Medicine, Master of Surgery. As if it was a premonition, on their graduation ceremony, the dean's address was about "The Evils of Malpractice in the Medical Profession".

As a college student, it was notable that Thomas was fond of chloroform (as well as other medications which could desensitize people); in fact, his thesis was about this particular substance. Not one of his fellow students and instructors noticed that Thomas would soon use his medical knowledge to kill. For them, he was just a polite man, who had was held in high regard when it came to wealth and appearance.

Shortly after graduation, Thomas was thrown into a hasty, at gun-point kind of marriage. Reports said that he stayed in the hotel owned by the Brooks family from Waterford, and in his time there he had a brief affair with one of the female members, Flora. After falling pregnant (supposedly to Thomas), Flora underwent an abortion at the hands of Dr. Cream, then an intern.

Flora's family searched for Thomas, complete with guns and threats that he must marry her. The doctor conceded, but as soon as the honeymoon was over (and experts doubt there was even one), the aspiring physician left a note on their bed, telling his bride that the best he could do for her was to "keep in touch".

From Canada, Thomas went to London, England to further his medical studies. Waterford served him well, but all the opportunities had been exhausted and it was time to move on and Britain was the best place to start over. During that time, areas like Glasgow, Manchester, and London was falling to pieces.

All around, you could see impoverished families (both native and migrants) and dead corpses lying in their bed - their demise caused by numerous reasons from hunger to sexually transmitted diseases. Because of these dire conditions, Britain sought to develop their medical care. They established the best medical schools and demanded that their doctors be not only geniuses, but also good-hearted.

Dr. Thomas Neill Cream definitely filled the first criterion, but not the second. However, it was hard to determine if a person had the ethics required of a doctor, so when he entered St. Thomas' Hospital in Lambeth, people around him were blinded by his supposedly extensive knowledge and skills as a foreign physician who graduated from the infamous McGill's.

After studying in yet another commended institution (the one that produced Florence Nightingale and Thomas Lister), Dr. Cream was accepted into the Royal College of Physicians and Surgeons, and soon enough, he earned his midwifery degree.

His Love and Hate For Women

As if his passion for medicine died down a little after conquering another degree, Thomas' attention shifted to women, particular those who came from the West End, where poverty was unheard of. In Westminster, the townhouses showed no sign of illness or hunger; people were busy with booming businesses or career.

And because he had good looks and a promising profession, Thomas didn't find it hard to be a lady's man-as long as he posed as a single man. Perhaps it was the place itself, or maybe it was because of his conservative upbringing and schooling, but Thomas found London to be a paradise where he could indulge in the pleasures of the flesh.

However, when Thomas discovered that not only well-bred female Londoners were in the area (there were also prostitutes), he was caught between desire and "righteousness". The man in him was probably titillated, but the psychosis residing in his mind was appalled- how could such creatures, who did nothing but offer themselves in exchange of a few pennies, exist? An idea then formed into his mind: he must do something about these women.

Later on, it would be revealed that Thomas' desire to kill could have started way before he reached London. In 1877, Flora, his wife from Waterford, Quebec, died of consumption (which meant tuberculosis). Although it was a natural cause, experts found out that before Thomas left in 1876, he had provided Flora with unknown medications.

Dr. Phelan, the doctor who examined the woman, suspected that he (Thomas) must have contributed to his wife's demise. With Flora out of the picture, Thomas Neill Cream, doctor emeritus, was single again, and he was set to "take care" of the women he despised so much.

While most serial killers and spree murderers today use either guns or knives, back in the Victorian age, the easiest way to kill was to purchase poisons. Frightening as it was, dangerous substances such as arsenic and laudanum were available over the counter. Strychnine, one of the most lethal, was sold with more caution, but if you were in the medical profession, it would be handed out to you without question - it just needed to be recorded. With this knowledge, Thomas became complacent. Killing women would be easy, but he would bide his time.

Whatever stopped him from pursuing a career in the United Kingdom remains unknown, but after finishing his studies, he went back to Canada in 1878 to practice his degree as a doctor and as a surgeon. In London, Ontario, Thomas set up his clinic in Dundas Street, right above Bennett's Clothe Store and for almost a year, he did quite well - after all, his credentials were appealing.

However, in 1879, a patient named Kate Gardener was found dead behind the building where his clinic was - the cause of death was chloroform poisoning. Further investigation revealed that Kate was an unmarried woman, but she was pregnant. Afraid of what the repercussions would be, she sought the expertise of the new doctor in town - Dr. Thomas Neill Cream.

When questioned, Thomas admitted that Kate had gone to him to ask for abortifacients, but he refused - he told the pregnant woman that suicide would be better, and that she could use chloroform because it was easily available in the market. The law authorities, however, didn't believe him.

For one, no bottle of chloroform was found near the area

where the body was found, if it was truly suicide, then, the pills would be there. Second, Kate's face was covered with scratches, as if she had been forced to ingest the poisonous pills.

The case developed from suicide to murder, and although the doctor was not indicted, his reputation was forever ruined. He needed to find a new territory.

Dr. Cream in Chicago

Hoping to escape the heat from the controversy, Thomas decided to head out to Chicago. He was expecting to see a humble place damaged by a huge fire, but he got a surprise when he noticed that it was now a city filled with career opportunities, brick houses, and busy streets. However, something sinister lurked in the city - politicians seized the opportunity to corrupt and authorities were incompetent in enforcing the laws. During that time, Chicago was hailed as the "wickedest city of the world" and Thomas would live up to its standards.

After passing the state board health exam (as he was originally from another country), Thomas resided in 434 West Madison Street for a short period of time. Albeit brief, his stay in the city as an abortionist became memorable - but not exactly good, at least not for the victims. The only problem was that the suspicions about him surfaced long after he went away.

One of the reasons for this was the crimes of others. In the 1880s, a lot of physicians (quack ones) tended to perform abortions, in and out of their clinics. At some point they even did it door to door - visiting the patient after office hours and bringing the equipment with them. Many of the patients were left bleeding to death due to the doctors' incompetence and greed.

Thomas was a full blown doctor, so suspecting him didn't quite make sense at that time, but unknown to them, should a patient succumb due to the procedure, he wouldn't feel bad about it.

Through the years, Thomas nurtured his hatred for fast women - his feelings were confused. Obviously he was enthralled by them (at least sexually) for he carried pornographic photos with him, but on the other hand, he also felt vulnerable. Experts reported that when in the company of prostitutes, Thomas would not be able to achieve erection without the help of aphrodisiacs, which he, himself, concocted. In their opinion, the women ultimately became a symbol of his sexual inability.

His perplexed attitude toward women was further reinforced by his experience as an abortionist. As he accepted pennies for his service, he developed this idea that women were cheap. That since they became pregnant out of wedlock (as most cases were), their death would account for nothing - should they die during the procedure, then, they only got what they deserved.

His hatred exhibited as he became less careful in his practice: instead of abiding to two goals (end the pregnancy and let the mother live), he only held to the first one. This carelessness almost landed him in prison when patient Mary Anne Faulkner died in his hands. However his up and coming lawyer insisted that the culprit was one of the midwives Thomas had hired, and that his presence there was to save the lady. For the second time after the death of Kate Gardener, Thomas escaped indictment.

Growing bolder with his malpractice, Thomas killed another woman named Ellen Stack after he prescribed her with "anti-pregnancy" pills. In her death, it was revealed that the pills were laced with strychnine, but the police were not able to link it back to Thomas.

His luck, however, ran out when he killed a man named Daniel Stott. According to an internet biography of Thomas (written by John A. Piper and Stephen P. Ryder), Daniel Stott was a railway agent plagued by epilepsy. Like so many others affected by this illness, he wished for the suffering to stop. So when he heard from fellow sufferers that an effective elixir was being sold by a certain Dr. Thomas, he immediately bought a bottle.

And it was effective; in fact, Daniel bought the medication regularly, until one day when he couldn't go to the doctor's clinic. In that instance, he sent his wife, Julia to pick up the elixir, but the woman received much more from the doctor: they had an affair. When the time came that Daniel learned of the illicit relationship, Dr. Cream laced his medication with strychnine, ultimately killing him.

Afraid that the death would be traced back to him, he wrote a letter to the coroner, informing them that the pharmacist had mixed the poisonous strychnine into the drug. The coroner refused to believe the accusation (mainly because the pharmacist had a spotless reputation) and a warrant for the arrest of Dr. Thomas Neill Cream was issued.

Upon hearing this, Thomas went back to Canada, but was captured and bought back to Illinois. After his trial, and after Julia Stott stood against him to save herself, the court sentenced him to a life in prison in Joliet State Penitentiary.

Julia's betrayal apparently triggered something even

darker in Thomas, for when he was released (using "crooked means" to gain a pardon) 10 years later in 1891, his hatred for the all womanhood reached its peak.

Vengeance

The "crooked" ways by which Thomas gained his freedom consisted of two things. First, his brother, Daniel, who had notable political influence, demanded leniency for his brother and secondly, the political and justice system during that time was very corrupt.

As quoted by Henri le Caron, a former Joliet employee, "Money could accomplish anything, from small to big luxuries in prison, to a pardon."

Aside from the hatred for women which he garnered after losing 10 years of his life, Thomas also received a huge sum of $16,000 which was his inheritance from his father (this is approx. $415,000 in today's money). Although a portion of it was spent on his pardon, a lot was still left - more than enough for him to start another life in London.

Because of this inheritance and the moral obligation to thank his brother, he went back to Canada first. In his stay there, it was obvious that Thomas had been through a lot. His life in prison showed in his every action - from his rattled speech, balding head, wobbly gait, grown mustache, frequent headaches and wrinkled face. A man of 40, Thomas looked older. His brother's wife was irritated by his presence, but not because of his ex-convict status, but because of the low-brow remarks he bestowed upon all women.

So, in September of 1891, when Thomas departed the Canadian land, Daniel's wife couldn't be happier.

Upon his arrival on British soil, he moved to 103 Lambeth Palace Road, in the south of London. It was a familiar place for him because it was where he had stayed during his St. Thomas Hospital School days. Shortly after moving, he realized that the headaches he had been experiencing since his release were not getting any better, in fact, they seemed to be worse.

His vision was also blurring, so he made an appointment to have it corrected - the optician gave him a pair of spectacles. Although it corrected his eyesight, the headaches persisted to the point that he needed to take a low dosage of morphine. Headache and hyper-myopia or not, nothing could stop him from eradicating the evil creatures called women.

His new look, which consisted of a balding head, a slightly limping gait, and a pair of eyeglasses, proved to be useful for Thomas. According to him, this new appearance would make women trust him more - the way a student trust his teacher. Sure, he wasn't as good looking as he was before, but he no longer desired to be lady's man - he wanted to be their executioner.

The first victim was Ellen "Nellie" Donworth, 19 years old, a former factory worker turned prostitute in the streets of Lambeth. In 1891, the same year Thomas left Canada and moved to Lambeth Palace road, Nellie moved in with a soldier Ernest Linnel. No one knows if the two were having a relationship, but reports said Ernest didn't mind the type of work Nellie did - so sharing a room together was acceptable.

On the evening of October 13, 1891, Nellie left the apartment telling the cleaning lady, Anne Clements, that she was going to see a gentleman whom she had recently met.

One friend, Constance Linfield, noticed Nellie with a well-dressed gentleman, however, knowing the lady's profession, she didn't pay them much attention. Later in the night, another friend, James Styles, saw Nellie standing at Morphet Place, alone and in pain. James assumed that she was drunk and had fallen somewhere, so he helped her back to her lodgings.

In the room, Nellie kept writhing in pain and had labored

breathing. She also kept telling her roommate Ernest, charwoman Anne, and friend, James, that the gentleman she was with gave her a drink of "white stuff". As Ernest and Anne attended to the helpless teen, James went away to fetch a doctor. Upon their arrival, Nellie was already uncontrollable - she couldn't breathe, and her spasms were so severe that restraint was impossible. The doctor immediately diagnosed the case as systemic poisoning, so they transferred her to St. Thomas Hospital, however, on the way, Nellie died.

The police report revealed that there was a lethal dose of strychnine in her stomach, and worse, they informed her family and friends, that her last hours were excruciating. From Angus McLaren's *Prescription of Murders*, it was explained that once a person was poisoned with strychnine, his mental capacity wouldn't be affected - he would be aware of everything that was happening.

That meant that Nellie was cognizant of every convulsion, spasm, and pain - she knew that she was dying with every painful intake of breath. The cause of death would be anoxia (lack of oxygen) because the patient's lungs would contract, hence, breathing becomes impossible.

The second unfortunate soul was that of 27 year old Matilda Clover. Like Nellie, she too lived in Lambeth Road and also made a living as a prostitute. She shared her home at No 27 with her 2 year old son, the landlords, Mr. and Mrs. Vowles, and the house helper Lucy Rose. Her son's father had abandoned them - the main reason why she was forced to work in the streets.

The week before she became one of Thomas' victims, she went to a doctor to curb her alcoholism: her prescription consisted of potassium bromide, an anti-convulsant and a sedative.

On the night of October 20, a cheerful Matilda left her home in 27 Lambeth - Lucy could only guess that it was because of her new acquaintance, Fred. According to the helper, while cleaning Matilda's room, she saw a note which instructed Matilda to meet the man, on the condition that she would be clean and sober.

By 9 pm, the young mother returned home with someone whom Lucy could only assume was Fred, and the two probably had a drink or two because Matilda went out to get some ale. Lucy wasn't certain of the time, but she could attest that the man (with unclear features due to the darkness) left alone.

By 3 am, the entire household was awoken by Matilda's screams: she was clutching the bedpost, writhing in pain, all the while screaming that Fred had given her poisonous pills. Doctors were called, but Matilda couldn't be saved -

she died in the morning of October 21 around 7:00 am.

Unlike Nellie's death, Matilda's wasn't declared as murder. In fact, the doctor who had assessed the 27 year old attested that her patient must have mixed alcohol and potassium bromide together; the combination, according to him, was lethal. Why they chose to dismiss Matilda's screams about the poisonous pills from a man named Fred remained unknown, but the police would soon discover that a serial killer was roaming Lambeth.

The Irony that was Dr. Cream

It was late October when Thomas killed Matilda Clover, and for a while, it seemed like his need for murder died down. In the coming months, he would be busy with the sophisticated Laura Sabbatini. As hard it was to comprehend, Thomas wanted to start a family with this lady, so he spoiled her.

Aside from accompanying her and her blind mother to London, taking them to the most elegant of restaurants, the doctor also shelled out enough money for Laura to establish her dream business: a dress enterprise. On January 2, 1892, however, Thomas had to go back to Canada to make the final arrangements for his father's inheritance.

Thomas returned to London in April of 1892, 4 months later after everything was taken cared of. He stayed in Hertfordshire, Laura's home, for a day to arrange their engagement. Upon returning to London, he proceeded with his nightly prowls yet again. His next supposed victim was Louise Harris, another prostitute, but unlike Nellie and Matilda, Louise was smart - she even provided Thomas with a fake name, Lou Harvey.

In their brief encounter, the serial killer noted how pale Lou's cheeks were, so he prescribed her with certain pills, which he handed out right away. Feeling something was wrong, Lou took the pills, but didn't swallow them - she discarded them when the gentleman turned away.

On April 11, two other victims were killed: prostitutes Emma Shrivell and Alice Marsh. Unfortunately, they hadn't been as smart as Lou, for when the good doctor offered them a box of gelatin-pills, they gladly accepted it and took it before the gentleman left. The two of them, of course, died the morning after.

After Emma's and Alices' murders, the "Lambeth Mystery" became clear: there was a poisoner lurking in the area.

Captured

Interestingly, the way Thomas was captured was similar to the way he was identified as Daniel Stott's killer: he tried to frame innocent people. As the heat of the Lambeth Mystery intensified, Dr. Cream sent a letter to the law authorities disclosing the names of Matilda Clover's killer. The police found it odd - Matilda's case wasn't listed as murder, so how did this doctor learn of the details?

His capture was sealed when a policeman from New York arrived in London and got in contact with Dr. Cream. The police had apparently heard of the Lambeth Mystery and inquired if Thomas knew something about it. Dr. Neill didn't disappoint - he gave the policeman a vivid explanation of the murders.

When the New Yorker told a British policeman of this seemingly knowledgeable doctor, Scotland Yard placed Dr. Cream under surveillance. Furthermore, they called the authorities in the United States where he originally came from and they learned of his poison-murder case back in 1881.

The rest, after that, was history.

On July 13, 1982, Dr. Thomas Neill Cream was charged with Matilda's murder. From October 17 to 21, his trial took place, and less than a month after, on November 15, he was hanged on the gallows of Newgate Prison. As a tradition, his body was laid in an unmarked cemetery inside the prison, and as if insulted by his crimes, McGill University removed his name from their list of graduates.

Chapter 2: The Diet Hazzard

We believe today's diets are rigorous and harsh, but only a century ago, many people voluntarily signed up to an even more gruesome treatment.

A pair of sisters from England were always on the hunt for the latest alternative treatment. The two spinsters, Claire and Dorothea (Dora) Williamson, were skeptical of traditional medical treatments and cures, and did not approve of drugs and medical procedures. They had given up wearing corsets and eating meat, all to improve their health.

Their family, on the other hand, did not approve of their quests in search for alternative cures. So when the sisters saw a newspaper ad, promising cures for every possible ailment, they packed their bags and didn't tell anyone they were leaving the Empress Hotel in British Columbia to try a new treatment in Olalla, Washington.

The institute they saw in the ad was situated in the countryside, leading the sisters to believe they would be spending their time gazing at the colorful sunsets and watching the beautiful horses run through the fields. They'd been expecting to eat the freshest fruits and vegetables from the nearby farms and being taken care of by the most caring medical personnel.

They were not seriously ill and did not suffer from any life-threatening disease. Dora had been complaining of rheumatic pains and swollen glands, while her sister was told she had a dropped uterus. They were daughters of a well-off army officer, so even if the alternative treatment was expensive, they could afford it.

The two young women arrived in Seattle in February, 1911 to undergo what was advertised as "the most beautiful treatment". But when they tried to sign up for the treatment, they were told that the institute in Olalla was not yet ready to take on patients. Instead, they were set up in an apartment in Capitol Hill. The pair started with the treatment immediately.

They were fed only two cups of broth a day and were massaged vigorously. The massage was forceful and painful, and the broth was strained and did not have any vegetables in it, only water. Every day, the patients had to endure 8 hour long enemas in a bathtub, which often made them faint and remain unconscious for the rest of the cleanse.

Two months later, the Williamson sisters were transferred to the promised sanatorium in Olalla. By that time, they both only weighed around 70 pounds. Their family could not intervene because the sisters left for their treatment secretly. Luckily, their childhood nurse, Margaret Conway, got a mysterious cabled massage, probably sent by one of the nurses, while she was visiting her family in Australia.

The message included only a few words which set off alarm bells in Conway's mind. She bought a boat ticket to the Pacific Northwest to visit the sisters. On the way to check up on the sisters, Conway heard the upsetting news: Claire had died. On the spot, she was explained that Claire died as a result of a course of medications she had received as a child.

Allegedly, the medications caused her internal organs to shrink gradually, which caused cirrhosis of the liver. According to the doctor responsible for administering the treatment, her health was already declining when they started the treatment.

Although Conway was not a licensed doctor, she knew something was wrong when she saw Claire's body. She was so undernourished; her skin stuck to her bones, her hair color was changed, and she looked like a skeleton. When she visited Dora, she couldn't recognize her. Her facial shape was unrecognizable and bones were sticking out beneath her clothes.

She could barely sit down because every bone in her body hurt. Even though she was clearly starving and feeling sick and her sister had already succumbed to the treatment, Dora refused to leave the clinic.

The horror did not end there. Later, Conway found out that the clinic's doctor had been appointed as executor of Claire's estate. Dora had signed a document which gave power of attorney to the doctor's husband. The malicious couple had legal rights over the sister's sapphires, diamonds and other valuable jewelry, their household goods, and clothes. The doctor in charge even explained Dora's mental and physical health while wearing one of her dead sister's dresses.

Behind the Fasting Fad

The mind behind the controversial treatment was Dr. Linda Hazzard. She was born in 1867, in Minnesota. Although she had some experience as an osteopathic nurse, she lacked a medical degree to start her own medical practice. However, by taking advantage of a loophole in the Washington law, she gained a license to practice medicine and take on patients as a fasting specialist.

Her degree described Linda Hazzard as a doctor of

osteopathy (one who can massage the joints, bones, and muscles). As such, she was able to open a sanatorium in Olalla- the well-known Wilderness Heights which was later renamed as Starvation Heights by the locals because starved patients from the sanatorium often walked around, some even begging for food from the nearby neighbors.

Linda and Samuel got married right after Hazzard's first victim died. Samuel was a known alcoholic, lecher, and a fraud, who was married twice before Linda. He never divorced either of his wives, so he was sentenced to two years in prison for bigamy. He pursued a career in the military from where he was discharged because he misappropriated military funds.

As they said, they were a match made by anything other than heaven.

The English sisters were not the only patients in the sanatorium, nor was Claire the only one who died. Before her, at least 13 other deaths were reported in the sanatorium, between 1908 and 1911. Hazzard performed autopsies on all of them, and there was always an underlying condition that caused their death.

However, only the medical documents of Daisey Maud Haglund proved she had stomach cancer, while the rest of the cases were declared as death caused by cirrhosis or starvation. One patient, Eugene Stanley Wakelin died on Hazzard's property from a bullet in the head. Suspicions still arise around this incident, and many believe the Hazzard couple may have killed Wakelin.

The diary of one of the patients presented the Hazzard starvation treatment best. It showed that the regimen included only tomato broth, oranges, or orange juice. He was fed only once or twice a day for several weeks, until he was taken to the Seattle General Hospital, where he died. The protocol for each patient was different and in accordance with their ailment. Some patients were starved only several weeks, while others had to go through the process for a couple of months straight.

In 1908, Hazzard wrote a book entitled "Fasting for the Cure of Disease". In her book she described her beliefs that starving the body to a virtual death cleanses it from toxins. She believed that the digestive system needed to rest and recuperate in order to eliminate impurities, even cancer cells. In her ideas, she was convinced that she could starve the body and rebuild it to health.

She was not the only doctor at the time to promote fasting as a method of cleansing the body, but none did it as rigorously as Hazzard did. The general public during that time believed fasting methods to be a quack treatment, but as a published medical textbook author, Hazzard was able to convince many people into trying her treatments. Some of them survived and publically praised her practice and notorious methods.

But her glory didn't last for long. When her patient Claire died, and her childhood nurse witnessed the health condition of Claire's sister Dora, she immediately informed the family. An uncle of the sisters, John Herbert was summoned to come over to the Wilderness Heights to manage Dora's release from the sanatorium.

He had to pay Hazzard a thousand dollars to free her from the infamous property. Later, in the trial against the starvation doctor, Dora testified against her. A rumor circled that Hazzard allied with the Butterworth mortuary and switched Claire's body with another skinny skeleton before her childhood nurse arrived to visit them, to avoid bringing suspicion on her methods and obviously underfed body.

The Hidden Agenda

Hazzard firmly believed in her methods of healing. She was known to call herself a gifted and brilliant healer and as a proud holder of a medical degree, she refused to be addressed as anything less than a Doctor. At her trial, she snapped at reporters who called her Ms. Hazzard, pointing out that Ms. Hazzard was her mother-in-law, not her.

Some believed she was ahead of her time, by challenging the medical establishment and creating new methods of alternative healing. Several deaths later, she was arrested.

Finally, on August 15, 1911, the authorities from Kitsap County arrested her on the charges of first-degree murder for the death of Claire Williamson. Her trial started in January the following year, when crowds gathered to hear about the methods of the despicable doctor.

Other than Dora, several nurses who worked at the sanatorium described the scandalous treatments. They told the court that the Williamson sisters cried in pain while Hazzard made them go through long hours of extensive enema, bath cleanses until the skin starts to scald and nutritional plans that scared even the most courageous faddist.

She refused to take any responsibility for the death of Claire Williamson. According to her book and her convictions, a death of the body has nothing to do with the starvation itself. Many of her patients who died under her methods were going to die of a certain condition soon anyway. She, like any other doctor, was only trying to heal them.

According to her, she was persecuted because she was a successful woman in a fraternity of men. Other alternative practitioners took a stand for her; some even offered support during her trial.

The prosecution called "financial starvation" came in second. It was determined that Hazzard forged letters, checks and conducted other types of frauds to help her empty the Williamson estate. The jury stayed indifferent to her claims of politically driven persecution, so they came back with a verdict very quickly.

She was sentenced to 2 to 20 years of hard work in prison in Walla Walla penitentiary. Although sentenced for only one murder at the time, Hazzard today is linked to the deaths of at least a dozen wealthy individuals who signed up for her program. One was even shot in the head, and while Hazzard claimed it was a suicide, it was established that she drained all his funds and administered his estate.

The Final Days of the Torturer

Linda Hazzard came out of prison after serving only two years. She fasted during her time there, to prove the value of her medical regimen. The governor, Ernest Lister, gave her a full pardon the following year. Although her medical degree was revoked and she never tried to reinstate it, together with her husband Samuel, she moved to New Zealand to continue her practice among supporters.

In 1920, she moved back to Olalla, where she opened a new sanatorium, known as a "School of Health". Because she lacked a medical degree, she was not licensed to practice medicine, but continued to supervise fasting patients.

In 1935, the new sanatorium burned to the ground and was never reconstructed. A few years later, Hazzard fell sick and tried to restore her own health with one of her fasting methods. She died shortly after, in 1938, in her early 70's.

Chapter 3: The Moorhouse Murders

On February 16, 1951, the eldest son of the Birnie family was born. He was named David. The family lived in Wattle Grove, a semi-rural suburb in east Perth. In the following years, David got 4 new brothers and sisters, but wasn't very happy about it because in the Birnie family, the oldest was responsible for the younger ones.

Once, David's brother broke something that belonged to their mother, so she chased David around the house with a broom. Their mother was an alcoholic - recognized by her vulgar behavior, language and manner. She was known to provide sexual favors to taxi drivers in exchange for cab fares.

Her neighbors said her youngest were always hungry, crying and wet. She was often seen riding in the school bus, where she would pass her baby to the person next to her (and not politely, she tended to use bad language), then take out her comics and cigarettes and enjoy the ride to wherever she was headed to.

The Birnie house was filthy and chaotic. In their home, a family dinner was never prepared, nor was any other meal. The fridge was always wide open so that the Birnies children and the family dog could eat whatever and whenever they liked. David's father was a frail man of very small build and had an arched back, probably from a genetic defect.

He was not an alcoholic, but he was rarely home, because he was working long hours to provide for the family. Rumors started spreading that the family had engaged in incest. Parishioners, neighbors, and friends said they were an irresponsible, unstable and dysfunctional family.

The local priest didn't want to marry them, stating that no good can come from that kind of pairing. The social workers often took one of the children to a government institution because the family was not able to take care of them.

In the early 60's, the family moved to another Perth suburb, where David found a true friend; her name was Catherine and she was only a few months younger than him. Catherine's mother died when she was only 10 months old. She was transferred to her father's, in South Africa, but moved back to her maternal grandparents a couple of years later when he realized he couldn't cope with her.

Her grandparents didn't love her a great deal either, and she was relocated back and forth during her early childhood. When she was 10 years old, her father, Harold, won sole custody over her. She was a sad little girl without friends, desperate for love and affection.

Other kids were not allowed to play with her, probably because of the environment she came from. She formed a strong bond with David and started a relationship with him when they were 14 years old. Her father tried to break the couple apart, but they only grew stronger.

Bonnie and Clyde-Like Rampage

As the couple grew, they started spreading violence and fear in the small peaceful suburb areas in Perth. David was first institutionalized at the age of 8 for petty burglary and breaking and entering. By the age of 16, the couple was involved in multiple criminal offenses. House break ins, robberies, and car thefts become their regular routine. Because of their age, they were treated lightly in the courtroom.

At the age of 15, David became an apprentice jockey. His trainer, Eric Parnham, remembered the first time he visited the Birnie household; seeing that it was messy, dirty and chaotic, Parnham agreed to give a job to the sickly looking boy, together with accommodation at the local boarding house.

But soon afterward, David got himself in trouble again. The lady landlord complained that the apprentice jockey broke into her apartment and tried to rape her. Luckily, the landlord had a dog, and the dog went crazy when David attacked her, so he took off.

The felonious couple continued causing troubles. They visited the courthouse many times, but the court always looked at Catherine with pity and gave her probation periods. David on the other hand, went in and out of prison, reuniting with Catherine in another criminal riot every time he got out of jail.

The couple lived their lives carelessly and dangerously until they turned 20. Then, for the first time, Catherine went to jail. At that time, the couple had 53 offenses behind them.

In jail, the counselor helped Catherine break her dependence on David. After jail, she found a job as a housekeeper and married the son of her employer. They seemed happy and she gave birth to 7 children - however, their firstborn was run over by a car in front of her, which may have scarred her fragile emotional state even further. David married a girl the same year Catherine did, and they had a baby daughter.

The Happy Lifestyle Isn't For Everyone

Catherine took no pride in her married life and her children. She was seeing David for the last two years of her marriage and after 13 years of marriage, she left her children and her husband to be the evil sidekick all over again. This time, they were not underdogs; they were in the big league.

Soon after they reunited, the couple ran out of adventures. They were too old to land themselves in jail for petty criminal charges, so this time, David had a different adventure in mind: an adventure of a sexual kind.

He had suggested a threesome to his former wife, but after she joked around, suggesting a man for the threesome, David never mentioned the idea again. Catherine was wildly in love with him and she often said she would go to the ends of the earth to please him, which worked to David's advantage.

After their sex life reached a dead end, David planted the idea in Catherine's mind that she would achieve intense orgasms if she watched him while he raped another woman. At the time, David worked at a store for spare parts, where the young Mary Neilson came in to buy tires. He told her to stop by his house for a better bargain.

The Raping, Strangling and Murdering Spree Begins

Mary Neilson came to David's house on Moorhouse Street at October 6th, 1986. She was a 22-year-old psychology student who worked part time at a deli. As soon as Catherine welcomed her in their home, she realized the bargain was just bait. The couple held her at knifepoint and chained her to the bed. David raped her repeatedly as Catherine watched.

The couple drove to the Gleneagles National Park near Albany Highway in Bedfordale, where Mary was raped again and strangled with a nylon rope. He stabbed her body with a knife, knowing that would speed up the decomposition process. They buried her in a shallow grave and left the crime scene.

While in prison, Catherine spoke to a writer who wrote a book about female killers. Catherine told her that she and Dave had written a book, which they used as a blueprint for their murders. It would remain unknown if they had followed the "blueprint", but 3 more victims would die.

A few weeks after their first murder, the couple cruised the streets looking for their next prey. This time, they found Susannah Candy, a 15-year-old girl who still lived with her family. They picked her up and soon the knife held by Catherine was calling the shots. They bound her in the back seat and took her to their house, where they repeated the steps from their first rape.

Because Susannah was underage, they knew her disappearance would bring suspicions, so they made her write letters to her family, saying she decided to go to Queensland with friends. The couple kept her alive the next day, to be able to make a phone call to her family.

In his desire to make Catherine experience the thrill first hand, David asked her to come to bed. When Susannah saw both of them in the bed, she started screaming, so Catherine slipped sleeping pills down her throat to keep her quiet. When the girl dozed off, she strangled her - with David by the bed watching them.

Later in the investigation, she stated that she enjoyed strangling Susannah because she was a female, and females destroy and hurt males. She too, was buried near their first victim.

In less than two weeks, the luck ran out for Noelene Patterson. The malicious couple saw her standing beside her car because she had run out of petrol. They picked her up, tied her down, and with a knife at her throat, carried her to their bed.

Noelene was an attractive, successful, 31-year-old woman, working as a bar manager at the golf club in Nedlands. Their intent was to rape and kill her, like their other two victims, but David changed his mind and kept her hostage for three days.

Using a reverse psychology trick, she befriended David and wanted to talk him out of killing her. Catherine became insanely jealous and ran out of the house, only to come back with an ultimatum. She told David they would either kill her, or she will kill herself. David folded so they slipped a heavy dose of sleeping medications to Patterson.

When the medications started working, he strangled her; he thought she was special and not like the other girls they killed, so they buried her in another grave, away from the other two victims. Catherine said she felt great pleasure while throwing sand and dirt on her face while they were burying her.

Their appetite started growing, so their next victim was abducted only 5 days after the last one. On November 5th, 1986, 21-year-old Denise Brown was waiting for a bus, when the cruising couple laid eyes on her. Catherine was the one who decided who they would pick up, and she chose Denise.

Once chained to the bed and raped, the couple dosed her

with sleeping pills and forced her to make a phone call, saying she'd be gone for a few days. The next evening, they drove her to Wanneroo pine plantation, where David raped her in the car while waiting for the night to fall.

Once darkness fell over the forest, the rapist assaulted her again and cut her throat while he was raping her. They dumped her in a shallow grave, but the girl sat up. This time, David grabbed an ax from the car and split her skull open, with two strikes.

Their Last Attempt

On November 10, 1986, a half-naked girl came into the Fremantle supermarket. She was a 17-year-old girl named Kate. The police were called immediately, and she told them that a man and a woman tied her to their bed, where she was raped by the man while the woman was watching them.

The woman stimulated the man's testicles and anus while he assaulted her, and at one point, they talked about injecting cocaine into his penis. They kept her for 24 hours, forced her to make a phone call like the other girls, telling people she'll be gone for a few days.

At one point, the girl tried to make friends with Catherine and she succeeded, so Catherine untied her. When the doorbell rang and Catherine went out of the room, Kate sneaked out of the house, escaping from the window in the room where they kept her. She led the police to the house where she was taken and the police found the incriminating room.

Passion Behind Bars

The police arrested David and Catherine Birnie the following day. After hours of interrogation, the couple kept saying they knew nothing about any girls murdered or raped - they claimed that the girl voluntarily joined their sexual games. As night was approaching, one detective jokingly said that it's getting dark and they needed to grab shovels and dig the girls up.

To their surprise, David said "Okay, there are 4 of them." Catherine confessed right after the detectives told her David had admitted to the murders.

At the trial, they both pleaded guilty and were sentenced to life imprisonment on the count of four murders and one abduction and rape. Although the law at the time required them to serve 20 years before asking for parole, they were never granted conditional release.

When asked why he pleaded guilty, David responded that he owed a guilty plea to the families of his victims.

David served his sentence at the Fremantle Prison in maximum security, but because he was continually beaten up, he was kept in solitary confinement. They transferred him to Casuarina Prison, where he stayed until he hung himself in his cell, on October 7, 2005.

Catherine is still serving time in the Bandyup Women's Prison. The couple was never married, but Catherine changed her surname to Birnie by deed poll right after she left her husband. They asked to be married but the request was rejected. They were not allowed any form of contact other than correspondence.

They exchanged 2,600 letters, and Catherine corresponded with other infamous women killers as well. She became a head librarian in the women's prison and was not allowed to attend David's funeral. She applied for parole several times, but her papers were marked "never to be released".

Chapter 4: Robin's Fetish

On June 1, 1981, a maid from the Moonlit Hotel in Villa Park, Chicago reported to the manager that something smelled awful. At first she thought it was going to be a fleeting odor - one that would go away eventually - but as the day went on, the smell only worsened.

Afraid that guests would start complaining about it, the manager tracked down where the smell was coming from, and he found it in the vacant field at the back of the building. According to the manager, he was prepared to dispose of a dead body, but only one that belonged to an animal.

What he saw, however, was the body of a woman; the remains only consisted of bone fragments, and some skin, which was being eaten by maggots. The manager didn't think twice; he called the police.

When three detectives received the call, they were not surprised. That area of Chicago was a rundown place - the fast-food chains, bars and clubs, and junky shops were often filled with shady people: those who were looking for either drugs, quick sex, or both.

Upon arriving at the lot, the police instantly knew that they had a murder case. Not only was the woman gagged, but she was also handcuffed, her sweater was still on, as well as her underwear, but they were pulled down to her thighs. The socks she wore contained a few rolled dollar bills, indicating that it wasn't a robbery gone wrong.

In their estimate, the three detectives agreed that the woman had been there for quite some time now, judging by the decomposition - worse, they also believed that she was left there alive and only died when she succumbed to whatever the cause of her death was.

The police didn't waste time; after all, they needed to know the identity of the victim by obtaining fingerprints and teeth impressions, if they were still salvageable. They also needed to discover if the current scene was also the murder scene (or was it just the dumping scene), the time of death, and of course, the cause.

As the body was being prepared to be sent to Coroner Pete Seikman, the detectives came to the conclusion that since it was the first report, the body had recently been left at the location. The implication was that the culprits, in case there was more than one, were able to tolerate the decomposing body before they had the chance (or the sense) to dump it.

Inspecting the Missing Persons report was of no use, for no one had reported a missing prostitute (they thought the victim was one because of the rolled up dollar bills). They had to wait 2 weeks for the teeth impression and fingerprints analysis, but it was worth it - finally, the victim was identified.

She was Linda Sutton, 28 years old, a mother of two, and as expected, a prostitute. Postmortem examination revealed that she had been dead for three days, but due to the large wound on her chest (her left breast had been removed), the decomposition rate was increased.

8 months after Linda's body had been discovered, another woman turned up missing. A 35 year old waitress was abducted from her car, and after a thorough search, her body was found on an embankment. The condition oddly resembling Linda's corpse, complete with amputated breast.

Although the new case was publicized, the police asked the media to not include the removed breast in their reports. They planned on using that information for interrogation purposes.

Not even a week passed and another body was recovered. This time, the victim, a Hispanic woman who was wearing an engagement ring, was also raped and tortured, but her breast was not removed - it had only been badly bitten. Another difference from the two other corpses was the fact that the killer masturbated on the body.

It wasn't indicated how the psychiatrists arrived at such a conclusion, but they all figured that the man behind this murder was a family man, probably someone who loved animals, and was a respected person in society. At night, however, he turned dark.

On May 15, Lorraine Borowsky was innocently walking her way to the realtor's office where she worked, when someone kidnapped her from the parking lot. Her body turned up in Clarendon Hills Cemetery in Villa Park some 5 months later. Like the other victims, she too was raped repeatedly, and tortured. A wire wound around her chest was also used to amputate her breast.

Exactly 2 weeks after Lorraine was abducted and killed, Shui Mak became the next casualty. Reports said she was on her way home from their family restaurant in Streamwood and was in the car with her brother. When the two argued, her brother dropped her off - thinking that one of their relatives who were driving behind, would pick her up.

She never returned alive, though, for her body was recovered buried in a construction site. Like all the others, she too, was raped, tortured, and mutilated.

In June, another prostitute named Angel York was

abducted, but she had the fortune to survive. According to her report, a red van took her and inside, the men handcuffed and raped her before slashing her breast off and masturbating on the wound. Their last action was to cover her mutilated breast with duct tape, before dumping her body outside like a used bottle.

At this point, the police now knew that there was more than just 1 killer (it would explain the differences in the modus operandi), but Angel's description didn't help the identification of the serial killers. And so, the murders continued.

In August of 1982, Sandra Delaware, a prostitute, was found in the Chicago River - her hands were tied at her back, and her breast was mutilated. On top of being raped, she had also been stabbed and strangled.

A little more than a week later, the body of Rose Davis (31) was found - her injuries were similar to the previous victims, but the police agreed she suffered more because aside from being raped and strangled, she was beaten with a hatchet.

Around the same time Rose was abducted, Carole Pappas (42) also went missing - however her body would be found some 5 years later.

As the bodies piled up, so had the clues; the Behavioral

Science Unit of the FBI reported that the murderer was probably someone with a confused sexuality - he could be a closet bisexual and he could look a little effeminate. These characteristics, albeit interesting, were not that helpful; the police needed the identity, but so far, none of the physical evidences (which comprised mostly of bodies and wounds) led them to the perpetrator.

Until Beverly Washington was attacked, raped, and tortured, and she survived.

Beverly was only 20 when a man held her captive in his van - aside from the usual torture and sexual assault, the man also amputated her left breast and slashed her right breast before finally dumping her body on a railroad track.

She survived the attack and from her, the police were able to gain invaluable knowledge about the van's description, as well as the man responsible for her near-death experience.

The Horror Through the Eyes of Beverly Washington

On the day 20 year old Beverly was abducted, she was working (as a prostitute). According to her, a slender white man wearing a flannel shirt and square-toed boots approached her for her services and since he offered to pay her more than her normal rates, she agreed. Things went sour when the man with greasy brown hair and a mustache pulled out a gun and urged her to go inside the van.

After commanding Beverly to get naked, the killer handcuffed her and forced her to perform fellatio. The last thing Beverly remembered was the man holding some wires - she fell unconscious because the serial killer had forced her to take some pills.

She was dumped afterwards with her left breast gone and her right nearly so; someone saw her, brought her to the hospital, and she survived. When the police questioned her, she revealed that the van was just as Angel had described it to be - it was red. In her memory Beverly recalled tinted windows, wooden dividers inside, and a roach clip and feather hanging by the rear view mirror.

Under Investigation

The date of the first encounter was not clear - some said it was October 5, some said 20, and another one mentioned November 7, but on that day, the police saw a van which fitted Beverly's description to a tee. When the driver of the van was interviewed, however, he didn't fit the man with greasy brown hair and mustache - for an instance, his hair was red.

Eddie Spreitzer, the driver, confided that the van belonged to his boss, Robin Gecht, and with his help, the police were able to track down Robin's address. Upon seeing him, the police new that he was their man - from his hair and mustache, to his shirt and boots, but the man before them was confident.

He didn't seem nervous, so the police figured that either he was innocent, or he just truly believed that he was untouchable. With Robin calm, collected and cooperative, and the fact that the police still didn't have an arrest warrant, they let him go after a couple of questions.

With the possible man under their watch, the police went back to the surviving victims and asked them to pick out a photo of their assailant- they picked Robin Gecht. A superficial background check revealed that Robin had been arrested 3 years prior, but due to his "underground" connections, he was freed.

Eddie Spreitzer

Nearly 100% positive that their man was Robin, the police interrogated him and Eddie once more; while the first was notably collected, Eddie seemed to be on the verge of breaking down.

Not before long, Eddie admitted to their crimes, which didn't just include rape, torture, and murder, but also a random drive-by shooting. In his story, Eddie was the driver while Robin was the shooter: the incident killed one man and left another, paralyzed.

The first incident on the prostitute killing was with a black hooker- whom he believed was never found because Robin disposed of her body in the waters (exact location was not disclosed). Before her death, the prostitute was used sexually, mutilated (Robin also removed her breast), and was shot to the head. To weigh her body down, the killer used a bowling ball.

In his 78 page report, Eddie mentioned the sordid details of how Robin murdered his victims, including his sick habit of having sex with the severed breasts, but the main suspect was not backing down. The two of them were interrogated at the same time, but while Eddie spilled everything, Robin looked as if he had nothing to worry about.

His attitude clearly frustrated the police, and worse, when the two were placed near each other, Eddie became scared- so much that he started changing his stories. He told the police that Robin killed no one, and it was his girlfriend's brother, Andrew Kokoraleis, who was the killer.

With this new revelation, Robin remained undisturbed; he admitted to knowing Andrew, but it seemed like he wasn't going to pin him down the way Eddie did. When Andrew was brought into the interrogation room, he confessed to their crimes. With disturbing details, he told the police how they used different weapons, from polished ones like knives, to unconventional things like piano wires.

Their signature was to remove one or both of the woman's breasts. Lastly, Andrew said that he had been involved in the murder of at least 18 women- the details he provided matched what the police had in their files, so they were keen to believe that the crew had been cornered.

Although Robin still showed no sign of guilt, his actions with the other women (even his wife) sealed his situation as one of the killers. Reports said that Robin had a breast fetish- he would often ask the ladies he was with to let him poke their chest with needles or pins. His wife even recalled that Robin had a penchant in poking even the infected skin wound.

Just as the police thought they heard it all, another member of the killing crew came up- Tommy Kokoraleis.

The Rituals

According to Tommy, the 4 of them (Robin, Eddie, him and his brother, Andrew) organized a satanic crew. It wasn't rare during the 1980s, because a lot of people (especially teenagers) were attracted to the notion of "meeting" the devil himself- it was just that Robin and his "Ripper Crew" hiked the idea by about a hundred notches.

In his admissions, Tommy related about the "altar" covered in red cloth which Robin set up right in a room of their house. The walls were painted with black and red crosses, and whenever his wife left for her night shift work, Robin and the crew would worship the devil by an act of "communion"- that was, to eat the flesh they had obtained from their victims.

Tommy added: during the ritual, the 3 members would gather around the altar while Robin took portions of the flesh. He would then read several Bible passages before handing out a piece of flesh to each of them.

As the ritual went on, all of them would masturbate on the piece of human meat- when all were satisfied, they would eat the flesh as if it was the oscha. Tommy confided that he had been to at least a dozen of these rituals, and had also been there to witness 2 murders, but like his brother, and Eddie, he refused to pin Robin down.

Eventually, the police asked Tommy why they would do such a crime, and the slow-witted of the Kokoraleis brothers answered that Robin "could make them do anything", as if he was an all powerful god.

Further interviews revealed that other people too, were scared of Robin. Some even warned the police not to look him in the eye, for no matter how cruel the action was, he would be able to "command" you to do it.

Perhaps it was the reason why his wife, despite all the weird things he wanted her to perform, tolerated him. Through it all, the man remained adamant that he had no crimes to admit.

The Devil on Trial

In an attempt to escape trial, Robin Gecht pleaded insanity, but the jury, after having him examined by psychiatrists, deemed him mentally fit to stand. A mistrial happened, but it resumed on September of 1983, where the prosecutor showed every possible evidences, including the "altar", the rifle used for the drive-by shooting, and some satanic literature.

Above all these, they also found a trophy box in his house-this contained at least 15 pieces of breast flesh.

When Robin stood to defend himself, he only agreed to one thing- and that was in attacking Beverly Washington- but he denied everything else, including the rape, torture, and murders: he insisted that he didn't kill anyone.

Knowing that they couldn't charge him with murder unless there was physical evidence to link him to any of it (like DNA), the jury resorted to charging him with other crimes namely: rape, attempted murder, armed violence, aggravated battery, and sexual assault. The verdict was 120 years in prison.

The Fates of the Ripper Crew

For his confession, Tommy was sentenced to life in prison for the murder of Lorraine Borowsky. Reports said the punishment should have been death, but since he had been consistent with his statement, his verdict was decreased. Currently, the punishment was commuted and Thomas "Tommy" Kokorailes will be released in 2017.

His brother, for his admission in the rape and torture of Rose Davis, was sentenced to a lifetime in prison, but later on he retracted all his confessions- telling the judges that the police officers unethically treated him to the point of confession; according to him, they even provided him with all the information to confess about.

With his retraction, the jury had to decide whether to believe the police, or believe Andrew- in the end, they believed the law authorities, and sentenced Andrew to death. The defense team argued about this ultimate punishment, pointing out that if ever the client was truly guilty, then the crimes still wouldn't merit a death sentence.

It was going to be a long battle, especially since at that time, a lot of people were pushing for the death punishment to be abolished. More so after the anti-death penalty supporters heard that Andrew was viewed by a prison chaplain as a safe man who could still be rehabilitated.

Furthermore, the defense team insisted that the court couldn't prove premeditation, which was a primary criterion in giving out the death penalty. As a last ditch effort, Andrew's lawyers stated that their client had schizophrenia, which may or may not be true- the fact that a psychiatrist diagnosed him with personality disorder could mean that he was "vulnerable" to external influences, such as one permeated by Robin Gecht.

The jury didn't change their mind though, so in 1999, Andrew Kokoraleis gained the title of being the last man to be executed in Illinois.

Edward "Eddie" Spreitzer was also placed in death row, but in 2003, his sentence was commuted to a lifetime in prison.

What the Experts Feel

In an attempt to understand the murderers, Jennifer Furio, an author, sent them a letter which she hoped they would respond to. Fortunately, Robin and Eddie replied.

In Eddie's letter, he claimed that he didn't do a bad thing alone, and that the only reason he performed the crimes was because he was afraid of Robin's power, as well as his shotgun. Jennifer believed that Eddie was truly a sweet guy, who only succumbed under the influence of a more confident Robin, who apparently gave him a job and some unfulfilled promises.

Eddie was, according to the author, a weak target, someone who, due to his unhealthy lifestyle and upbringing, became easy for Robin to manipulate.

Eddie said that each attack they made was random- it wasn't planned: they would only have a target whenever Robin saw one woman with large bosoms, as he was very fond of it.

Robin's letter contained some answers as to why he was obsessed with women's breasts: he said that it was "a family thing", that every male in his parentage had a penchant for large breast.

Candidly, he reported in the letter that he was very satisfied with his former wife who had a chest measurement of 39D. Asked if he was guilty of the crimes, he insisted (as he had before), that he killed no one- he was not a serial killer.

Jennifer could only categorize him as a Mansonesque killer (from the Manson family famous for their murders), someone who could "encourage" people to do his bidding.

Chapter 5: Was Martha Guilty?

Martha Rendell was born on August 10, 1871, and in her time, Victorian rules still applied in her home town of Adelaide, South Australia. Martha grew up to be a rebel. At the age of 16, she left home to become a "free spirit", someone not bound by the priggishness of the era.

Along the way, she became involved with a number of different men, resulting in the birth of three children - all of whom were illegitimate. As if to mock the people who judged her lifestyle, she entered a relationship with a married man in the 1890s.

The man, Thomas Nicholls Morris, would make Martha abandon everything else, including her three children. In 1890, the gossip about their relationship was in full swing, and given Adelaide's strict observance for tradition, it was torture, especially for Thomas' wife and their 9 children.

Desiring to get away from everything, they headed to Perth, over 1600 miles away from Adelaide. Reports said that in Perth, the chance of starting anew appealed to the Morris family, on top of the fact that a good job was waiting there for Thomas.

In wasn't clear how she managed it, but Martha followed the family to Perth.

In the Name of Love

Like Adelaide, Perth was considered a "baby" town in the sense that it had only been incorporated in 1865, although its history dated back to the 1600s. When the Morris's and Martha arrived in Perth, development was at full swing - as well as factions distinguished by wealth.

These wealthy people would be the ones to push capital punishment for unforgivable offenses, something that Martha, herself, would be subjected to.

With a new environment and more accepting people (because no one in Perth knew of their affair), Martha and Thomas resumed where they had left off. As a domestic helper, Martha worked to provide not just for herself, but also for her lover's whims.

At this point, she wanted to make the relationship work, because if it didn't, then she didn't know where else to go. In Adelaide, she was a social pariah, and who could blame the people there? She had various affairs, had three illegitimate children, got involved with a married man, and then when said married man escaped, she followed - not once did she think about her children.

No, she would never go back to Adelaide.

On the surface, everything was going smoothly for the illicit lovers, but deep down, they were breaking to pieces. In Perth, women had more rights (especially in the area of voting), but much was also expected of them. On top of the high morale a woman would achieve if she entered a Christian marriage, she would also be encouraged to bear more children.

This was because of the significant decrease in population. The government needed to ensure that all the children would grow up to be upright citizens, so health both at home and in school, was reinforced. In simpler words, family became Perth's (and Australia's) powerhouse.

Although they claimed to love each other, Martha and Thomas would never be a family, especially since divorce was next to impossible. The state, especially in Perth, wholly believed that a Christian family should stay intact - if divorce was accepted, then the "floodgates" to adultery and orphaned children would open.

Divorce for Thomas would be expensive and scandalous. Should he pursue to it to be with Martha, then the Adelaide fiasco would happen all over again. Not much was known about Mrs. Morris, but some questioned her goodness as a wife and mother, especially so when Thomas finally left her in 1906.

No divorce happened, but Thomas abandoned her, took his 5 youngest children with him, and went away with Martha. Perhaps, he should have just left the children with his wife. She wouldn't be a good mother (although that was just a speculation), but perhaps, she wasn't capable of murder.

Which Martha was, as the court would suggest.

Not a Fairy Tale

Thomas, Martha, and the children moved to East of Perth, where the inhabitants were mostly transients. A good place because they mostly kept to themselves. In the few times that someone intruded on their affairs, Martha pretended to be Thomas' wife - if they didn't do it, they would be shunned.

After a couple of months, Martha realized how unhappy their life was: she stayed at home to do domestic chores, the girls were still too small to help her, the boys had school, and Thomas was away most of the time for work. Their home was also no more than a shack, and she developed no ties with her neighbors.

She was alone in the company of children that weren't even hers to begin with. Perhaps it was this that brought her to murder three of her stepchildren.

The story was quite simple, but it made Martha's status as severe as that of Belle Gunness. According to reports, Martha coated the children's throats with the "spirits of the salt" the traditional term for hydrochloric acid. This action made the children sick, so treatment was sought, but to no avail.

Due to the poisonous substance, their throats constricted - causing them to lose their appetite and making their intake of breath laborious. In short, their deaths became a result of starvation - a long, cruel process.

What made the situation worse was the fact that doctors thought it was diphtheria because the symptoms were similar. Hence, Martha was not suspected initially.

The first child to succumb was 7 year old Annie. She died in July of 1907, and the family physician listed her death as natural (diphtheria).

In October, 5 year old Olive followed, and like Annie, the cause of death was listed as natural (typhoid).

When in the next year 14 year old Arthur died, the family doctor, Dr. James Cuthbert, asked for Martha's permission to do an autopsy.

He figured that although diphtheria was a communicable disease, it was still a little strange that 3 children died in one household at different times. Martha agreed to the

Serial Killers True Crime

postmortem exam - she was even there when Dr. James did the procedure.

Nothing was found.

In April of 1909, George, 15 years old, complained of a sore throat after Martha gave him a cup of tea. Scared that he may somehow suffer the same fates as his siblings, he ran away and went back to his biological mother who was several streets away.

On that day, Thomas returned home - he noted George's absence, but did nothing to further search for him. Some of the neighbors asked him where his other son was, and when he directly replied that he didn't know, the concerned residents called the police.

How could they not when three children had already died in the household in the span of 2 years, and now one child was missing.

The Investigation and the Hasty Trial

Harry Mann, an inspector of police, was the first to arrive in the area when the report was received. While interviewing the neighbors, he found out that Martha was an indifferent caretaker. Apparently, if the children were screaming in pain, she would just ignore them. Others

63

also pointed out how she maltreated the girls, for an instance, young Annie, who was not able to walk for a while after one serious beating from her stepmother.

Finally, when inspector Harry found George, he was informed of the vicious truth: Martha Rendell was poisoning her stepchildren. It was true that George had no proof, but his suspicion could not be dismissed. The coroner started an investigation regarding Martha's actions around the time of the childrens deaths.

They found out that she had bought a notable quantity of spirit of salts. Stranger and more suspicious was the fact that the purchases stopped after Arthur died. In July 3, 1909, the court ordered that the bodies of the three children be exhumed, and in doing so, they discovered that their throat tissues were indeed lined with hydrochloric acid.

The public was outraged - not only because children were treasured during those times, but because women should never act the way Martha did. Thomas Morris was acquitted, but Martha Rendell, after deliberation from an all-male jury, was sentenced to death.

She became the last woman in Western Australia to be hanged. Interestingly, the date of her execution, October 6, 1909, was Arthur's death anniversary. Her grave can be found in Fremantle Cemetery.

Was Martha A Killer?

It was true that Martha Rendell was a lot of things. She was a rebel - someone who chose not to abide by tradition. One can even say that she was ahead of her time, even brave, but no one can deny that her morals were not becoming - even to today's standards. She left her children to pursue a man which was married to another woman.

If she did the same thing today, she would still be frowned upon, but certainly, not to the point of a "hasty" trial and execution.

Others claimed that Martha Rendell was not a killer - she was a victim. A victim in the sense that she was confined to live a bitter life, one where she needed to pretend to be Mrs. Morris when she really wasn't and had zero chance to be. She forced all her stepchildren to call her "Mother", because if not, their cover would be blown.

Perhaps there was some truth in her abuse (especially to little Annie as there were witnesses), but abuse during that time was common because it reinforced discipline. Martha's supporters (which were almost none during her time) claimed that she definitely wasn't mother material -

because she was pressured and bitter, living in a society where women like her were shunned.

But there was evidence to prove that she cared for the children. In 1907, all the 4 kids were diagnosed with diphtheria, and since Thomas was working, they were all left under Martha's care. The family doctor, Dr. James Cuthbert, even commended her for taking care of the children at the expense of her own health (but on trial he stood against her).

Health officials from the government also made a random visit to their household to "inspect" the health of the children (as a part of their health development goals), and all the kids were healthy - no abuse was detected.

All these, and the court's baseless evidence for the execution, made many people (after the fact) believe that Martha was innocent and was just a victim of a hateful society who thought differently than her. According to court records, the children died of constricted throats which caused the inability to eat and difficulty of breathing, but hydrochloric acid is not capable of that.

Too little will only irritate and too much would kill - so how did the children last that long? Martha was uneducated - she was far from being a chemist, so how could she have known the correct dosage for a crime to commence?

More notable was the idea that should Martha really want the children dead, she need not do anything. Diphtheria is a very fatal disease, especially when treatments were not as efficient - one small pop from the "whitish coating" in their throat could be toxic for a child.

And another interesting fact is the use of hydrochloric acid - back in Martha's days, self-medication was rampant. Even more so in families who couldn't afford the service of a doctor on a regular basis, and believe it or not, hydrochloric acid was an accepted antiseptic and was often used by mothers for "swabbing".

People argued that the reason why Martha purchased it was to treat the children, not to poison them. Put that way, the cessation in her purchases would also make sense after Arthur died.

However, Martha was not given the benefit of the doubt, and some authors said that it was because of her societal status - the moment the "poisoning" case was made public, her real relationship with Thomas was also revealed, and hence people started to view her as a social abomination. The woman who "stole" the husband of another and lived in sin.

They didn't take into consideration the fact that her

relationship with Thomas started in the 1890s and only ended in 1909 (when the issue surfaced), whereas the wife was abandoned by Thomas for an unclear reason. Sad as it was, some authors and experts believed that should Martha be a legal wife (and someone who socialized more), they might have viewed the events as "negligence" instead of murder.

Dr. James Cuthbert was questioned, and he too, turned his back on the woman, despite the fact that he had diagnosed Annie with diphtheria, particularly the symptoms cardiac weakness and epilepsy. Olive and Arthur were also diagnosed and Dr. James pointed out that it was typhoid.

Upon Arthur's autopsy, the doctor didn't find anything, but he implied that Martha stopped the procedure midway - this didn't bode well for her because it was viewed as an act of "hiding" the evidence. Martha insisted that she only stopped the postmortem exam because she believed that the doctor had scraped enough to get what he needed, but no one listened to her.

George, the 15 year old boy who ran away from home, was also an important factor in the case. His statement (especially his revelation of his father's and Martha's immorality) set the motion for the execution. Surprisingly so, it seemed he too lied. His story that Martha was trying to poison him with cups of tea was apparently fabricated, because long before the accusation, he was already living with his mother.

It was as if George wanted so much to be with his real mother that he was prepared to lie- even telling the investigators that his father was an accomplice. The surprising part was Thomas was acquitted because the jury thought that George had lied about his involvement. If they discounted George's statements against Thomas, why didn't they do the same thing for Martha?

They reasoned that Martha was the dominatrix in the relationship, and Thomas was too weak-willed to kill, and since the man was always at work, only Martha could perform the crimes. The most frustrating part of the trial (though some believed it was a forgone conclusion) was the "evidence" of hydrochloric acid in the children's throats.

Upon the court's announcement, people became outraged and their "need" to punish Martha reached an uncontrollable level. The fact was, the so-called evidence was fabricated. Medical practitioners attest that hydrochloric acid is a water-soluble substance.

That means that the prosecution team would not be able to "detect" its presence in a corpse, especially in Annie's who had died 2 years before the exhumation. If only her defense team was able to fight this "conclusive" evidence, Martha would have escaped execution.

Needless to say, Martha's trial was ever so hasty, and it seemed like she was persecuted not because of murder, but because she was herself - old, bitter, unhappy, unsociable, and immoral.

Conclusion

Thank you again for purchasing this book!

The investigation of a crime doesn't stop in the identification of the criminal - two teams have to battle the truth out in the courtroom. Complication arises when there is bias, conflict of interest, or lack of desire to discover the real events.

The prosecution team should aim to punish the accused, while the defense should prove his innocence. The jury should listen closely - the littlest of clues could bring out a significant discovery.

In other words, no trial should ever be short, unless one evidence (preferably physical) conclusively points to the killer. And even in its presence, the evidence should still be examined for authenticity.

In the 5 cases that we have discussed, do you think the truth won?

If you enjoyed this book, do you think you could leave me a review on Amazon? Just search for this title and my name on Amazon to find it. Thank you so much, it is very much appreciated!

Other Books Written By Me

Below you'll find some of my other popular books that are popular on Amazon and Kindle as well. You can visit my author page on Amazon to see other work done by me. (Travis S. Kennedy).

True Crime Stories

True Paranormal

True Paranormal – Book 2

True Crime

Serial Killers True Crime

True Ghost Stories And Hauntings

True Ghost Stories And Hauntings – Book 2

True Ghost Stories And Hauntings – Book 3

True Crime Stories – Book 2

You can simply search for these titles on the Amazon website with my name to find them.

LIBRARY BUGS BOOKS

Like FREE books?

Would you like them delivered to you every week?

Do you like non-fiction books on a huge range of different topics?

We send out FREE e-books every week so we can share our books with the world!

We have FREE books every week on AMAZON that we send to our email list. If you want in, then visit the link below to sign up and sit back and wait for new books to be sent straight to your inbox!

It couldn't be simpler!

www.LibraryBugs.com

If you want FREE books delivered straight to your inbox, then visit the link above and soon you'll be receiving a great list of FREE e-books every week!

Enjoy :)